BASEBALL LEGENDS

Hank Aaron
Grover Cleveland Alexander
Ernie Banks
Johnny Bench
Yogi Berra
Roy Campanella
Roberto Clemente
Ty Cobb
Dizzy Dean
Joe DiMaggio
Bob Feller
Jimmie Foxx
Lou Gehrig
Bob Gibson
Rogers Hornsby
Reggie Jackson
Shoeless Joe Jackson
Walter Johnson
Sandy Koufax
Mickey Mantle
Christy Mathewson
Willie Mays
Stan Musial
Satchel Paige
Brooks Robinson
Frank Robinson
Jackie Robinson
Pete Rose
Babe Ruth
Nolan Ryan
Mike Schmidt
Tom Seaver
Duke Snider
Warren Spahn
Willie Stargell
Casey Stengel
Honus Wagner
Ted Williams
Carl Yastrzemski
Cy Young

CHELSEA HOUSE PUBLISHERS

BASEBALL LEGENDS

DUKE SNIDER

Peter C. Bjarkman

Introduction by
Jim Murray

Senior Consultant
Earl Weaver

CHELSEA HOUSE PUBLISHERS

New York • Philadelphia

Published by arrangement with
Chelsea House Publishers.
Newfield Publications is a federally
registered trademark of Newfield
Publications, Inc.

CHELSEA HOUSE PUBLISHERS

Editorial Director: Richard Rennert
Executive Managing Editor: Karyn Gullen Browne
Copy Chief: Robin James
Picture Editor: Adrian G. Allen
Art Director: Robert Mitchell
Manufacturing Director: Gerald Levine

Baseball Legends
Senior Editor: Philip Koslow

Staff for DUKE SNIDER
Copy Editor: Catherine Iannone
Editorial Assistant: Kelsey Goss
Designer: Cambraia Magalhães
Picture Researcher: Alan Gottlieb
Cover Illustration: Daniel O'Leary

Library of Congress Cataloging-in-Publication Data

Bjarkman, Peter C.
Duke Snider / Peter C. Bjarkman; introduction by Jim Murray;
senior consultant, Earl Weaver.
p.   cm.—(Baseball legends)
Includes bibliographical references and index.
Summary: A biography of the gifted Brooklyn Dodger center-
fielder nicknamed the Duke of Flatbush.
ISBN 0-7910-1190-9
ISBN 0-7910-1224-7 (pbk.)
1. Snider, Duke, 1926– —Juvenile literature. 2. Baseball
players—United States—Biography—Juvenile literature.
3. Brooklyn Dodgers (Baseball team)—History—Juvenile
literature. [1. Snider, Duke, 1926– . 2. Baseball players.]
I. Title. II. Series.
GV865.S55B53 1992
796.357'092—dc20
[B]
                                                91-28903
                                                CIP
                                                AC

CONTENTS

WHAT MAKES A STAR

Jim Murray

No one has ever been able to explain to me the mysterious alchemy that makes one man a .350 hitter and another player, more or less identical in physical makeup, hard put to hit .200. You look at an Al Kaline, who played with the Detroit Tigers from 1953 to 1974. He was pale, stringy, almost poetic-looking. He always seemed to be struggling against a bad case of mononucleosis. But with a bat in his hands, he was King Kong. During his career, he hit 399 home runs, rapped out 3,007 hits, and compiled a .297 batting average.

Form isn't the reason. The first time anybody saw Roberto Clemente step into the batter's box for the Pittsburgh Pirates, the best guess was that Clemente would be back in Double A ball in a week. He had one foot in the bucket and held his bat at an awkward angle—he looked as though he couldn't hit an outside pitch. A lot of other ballplayers may have had a better-looking stance. Yet they never led the National League in hitting in four different years, the way Clemente did.

Not every ballplayer is born with the ability to hit a curveball. Nor is exceptional hand-eye coordination the key to heavy hitting. Big-league locker rooms are filled with players who have all the attributes, save one: discipline. Every baseball man can tell you a story about a pitcher who throws a ball faster than anyone has ever seen but who has no control on or *off* the field.

The Hall of Fame is full of people who transformed themselves into great ballplayers by working at the sport, by studying the game, and making sacrifices. They're overachievers—and winners. If you want to find them, just watch the World Series. Or simply read about New York Yankee great Lou Gehrig; Ted Williams, "the Splendid Splinter" of the Boston Red Sox; or the Dodgers' strikeout king Sandy Koufax.

A pitcher *should* be able to win a lot of ballgames with a 98-miles-per-hour fastball. But what about the pitcher who wins 20 games a year with a fastball so slow that you can catch it with your teeth? Bob Feller of the Cleveland Indians got into the Hall of Fame with a blazing fastball that glowed in the dark. National League star Grover Cleveland Alexander got there with a pitch that took considerably longer to reach the plate; but when it did arrive, the pitch was exactly where Alexander wanted it to be—and the last place the batter expected it to be.

There are probably more players with exceptional ability who didn't make it to the major leagues than there are who did. A number of great hitters, bored with fielding practice, had to be dropped from their team because their home-run production didn't make up for their lapses in the field. And then there are players like Brooks Robinson of the Baltimore Orioles, who made himself into a human vacuum cleaner at third base because he knew that working hard to become an expert fielder would win him a job in the big leagues.

A star is not something that flashes through the sky. That's a comet. Or a meteor. A star is something you can steer ships by. It stays in place and gives off a steady glow; it is fixed, permanent. A star works at being a star.

And that's how you tell a star in baseball. He shows up night after night and takes pride in how brightly he shines. He's Willie Mays running so hard his hat keeps falling off; Ty Cobb sliding to stretch a single into a double; Lou Gehrig, after being fooled in his first two at-bats, belting the next pitch off the light tower because he's taken the time to study the pitcher. Stars never take themselves for granted. That's why they're stars.

BIRTH OF A LEGEND

There is no such thing as instant immortality in baseball. A Hall of Fame career must be painstakingly earned, game after game, season after season. But now and then a diamond career—or at least a reputation—does seem to be created in a dramatic flash. Stardom may be conferred on a player with a single magical swing of the bat. This is the impression that remains with many fans, at least, even if the reality is more complicated.

Such was the case at Ebbets Field on October 1, 1952, during Game 1 of the World Series between the home-team Brooklyn Dodgers and the crosstown New York Yankees. The score was knotted 1–1 in the bottom of the sixth inning when Duke Snider, the Dodgers center fielder and cleanup hitter, came to bat with two men out and Pee Wee Reese, the Dodgers shortstop, standing on second base.

Snider had already enjoyed four solid big league seasons, averaging 98 RBIs and batting .298. But as he stood at the plate staring out at Allie Reynolds, the burly New York fireballer, Snider was not at all sure that he could bring Reese around. "I was about to find out," he recalled, "if I had the most important requirement of all to be a major-leaguer in the true

Duke Snider shakes hands with Dodgers manager Charlie Dressen as he rounds third base after clouting a two-run homer in Game 1 of the 1952 World Series. After hitting three more round-trippers during the seven-game Series, Snider said that he felt like "a real major leaguer."

definition of that term—the ability to succeed under pressure."

Snider had already appeared in the World Series, in 1949, and the experience had been a haunting disaster. The young phenom who had batted .292 with 23 home runs and 92 RBIs during the season had been a washout in October. While the Dodgers managed to win just one game against the overpowering Yankees, Snider batted a paltry .143, with no home runs or RBIs. Facing Reynolds in the first game of the Series, he had struck out three times and hit a weak pop-up.

But now, three years later, Snider was being given a second chance. Thinking that Snider would be overanxious, Reynolds started him off with a curveball that broke down into the dirt, but Snider wisely laid off it. Snider now had the edge in the endless cat-and-mouse game played by hitters and pitchers. He knew that Reynolds would come back with his bread-and-butter pitch, a rising fastball, and he was ready to start his swing a fraction of a second earlier. Reynolds cranked and fired. As the ball rocketed toward the plate, Snider thought it might be out of the strike zone, but he still believed he could handle it.

Snider whipped his bat into the pitch and made solid contact. The Brooklyn fans rose from their seats with the crack of the bat; even before the ball disappeared over the towering right-field wall, they had begun a joyful celebration. The Dodgers had a lead they would not relinquish, and Snider had erased the bitter memories of 1949. "I finally belonged," he later wrote about that moment. "I was a *real* major leaguer."

Unhappily for Brooklyn fans, the Yankees

rebounded to win yet another World Series, 4 games to 3. But Brooklyn's defeat was no fault of Snider's. He finished the Series as the leading hitter on both teams, with 4 home runs, 8 RBIs, and a .345 batting average. In Game 4, played at Yankee Stadium, he also made the fielding play of the Series, racing toward the center-field fence and leaping high in the air to spear a screaming line drive off the bat of Yankees first baseman Joe Collins.

In the half dozen summers to follow, Snider would reign as one of the biggest hometown heroes in American sports. His lasting reputation would be built upon doing exactly what he did on October 1—launching towering home runs onto Brooklyn's Bedford Avenue, which ran behind Ebbets Field's right-field wall. He did this so reliably that neighborhood youngsters began to station themselves on the avenue with their gloves, waiting for the Duke to hit one out.

Snider seemed destined for stardom in many ways, not only with his baseball talents but even with his nickname. In a sport that has always gloried in colorful monikers, none has ever been more natural than Duke, which creates an image of power, royalty, grace, and heroism. With his striking good looks and his elegance on the field, Snider definitely looked the part. He was the perfect baseball hero of the new television age. And for the boisterous, hardworking, ever-faithful fans of the Dodgers, he represented a style and grace that the average Brooklynite would usually see only on the silver screen at the neighborhood movie palace. It was fitting that Brooklyn's beloved Duke had begun life on the other side of the continent, in the land of palm trees and Hollywood stars.

Weary and disappointed, Snider towels off after the Yankees' 4–2 victory in the deciding game of the 1952 World Series. Despite Snider's 4 home runs, 8 RBIs, and .345 Series batting average, the Dodgers had lost their third Fall Classic to the Yankees in six years.

CALIFORNIA DREAMING

Baseball is full of stories about dedicated fathers who labored diligently to make major leaguers out of their children. Mickey Mantle's father spent endless hours turning his son into a switch-hitting wonder; Bob Feller's father built a complete ballfield on the family farm and provided the future Hall of Famer and his schoolmates with uniforms and a grandstand.

Edwin Donald Snider, born on September 19, 1926, in Los Angeles, California, was also blessed with a dedicated father who happened to be a former ballplayer. Ward Snider, a onetime outfielder with local semipro teams, had never made it to the major leagues or even the high minors. Throughout the Great Depression of the 1930s, he had been fortunate to find work with the Goodyear Tire and Rubber Company. He and his wife, Florence Johnson Snider, lived modestly with their only child in a small apartment at the back of a grocery store. When Edwin was only a toddler, his father put a ball and a bat in his hands and nicknamed him Duke—supposedly because the youngster acted like royalty around the house. Florence Snider never cared for the nickname and continued to call her son Edwin, even after the entire nation knew him as Duke.

Duke Snider as a member of the Compton Junior College basketball squad. As the leading scorer on the basketball team, the star quarterback on the football team, and a pitching phenom on the baseball diamond, Snider won 16 varsity letters during his high school career.

Duke later recalled that his father always had time for baseball; even on those afternoons when he came home from work exhausted, his hands blistered from a day of handling the hot molding equipment in the construction pits of the Goodyear plant. Ward Snider was never too tired to practice hitting and throwing in the backyard with his son. He insisted from the beginning that Duke—a natural righty—bat from the left side of the plate to gain an advantage, since most big league parks at the time favored southpaw swingers. Duke resisted, and he and his father would argue furiously, until Florence Snider called out, "You two children behave out there!"

When the Sniders moved to the Los Angeles suburb of Compton, Duke attended Enterprise Junior High School through the 10th grade and finished his high school education at Compton Junior College. He was a multitalented athlete at both schools, starring in football and basketball as well as his beloved baseball. As a quarterback, he led the Compton team to its first football championship in over 15 years, and he was also the top scorer on the basketball team. Altogether, he won 16 varsity letters in four years of high school play and was a member of city all-star teams in each of the three major team sports. His parents did everything to encourage him. Though they were always hard-pressed for money, they never asked Duke to get a job after school because they wanted him to be able to concentrate on sports. As long as he did his chores around the house, his free time was his own.

Duke's most memorable moments occurred on the baseball diamond. It was his pitching talent that first caught the notice of rival players and coaches, as well as the big league scouts who covered the local high school baseball circuit. In his first varsity game, the 15-year-old turned in a dazzling no-hitter, striking out 15 batters while collecting 3 base hits of his own.

At this time, Duke got a big boost from a Compton basketball teammate with a flair for writing and promotion. The youngster, Pete Rozelle, was at the time contributing reports on high school sports to the *Long Beach Press-Telegram.* In his weekly column, "Pete's Repetes," Rozelle extolled Snider's athletic feats. He also wrote letters to sportswriters on neighboring community papers, touting the sensational play of the Compton star. In later years, Rozelle became a major sports figure in his own right as the longtime commissioner of the National Football League.

Not only did Rozelle act as Snider's unofficial press agent; his uncle Joe was Duke's first official baseball coach. A later coach, Enterprise Junior High's Bill Schleibaum, also gave Duke's career a major boost. During Duke's sophomore year, Schleibaum wrote to Branch Rickey, president of the Brooklyn Dodgers, praising his young player's ability. Rickey was interested, and before long the Brooklyn scouts were on Duke's trail. By the time Duke reached his senior year, a whole herd of major league bird dogs were beating a path to Compton. One of them wrote in his scouting report, "Snider has steel springs in his legs and dynamite in his bat."

Duke Snider was not one to forget his friends. When Snider was inducted into the Baseball Hall of Fame in Cooperstown, New

Pete Rozelle, who eventually became a major sports figure as commissioner of the National Football League, was one of Snider's best friends in high school. Already a successful sportswriter, Rozelle used his talents to publicize Snider's feats on the athletic field.

York, four decades later, Pete Rozelle, his uncle Joe, and Bill Schleibaum were there for the ceremonies as honored guests.

Back in 1944, the Hall of Fame was no more than a fantasy for Snider, but the major leagues were a realistic hope. That spring, Brooklyn scout Tom Downey showed up at the Snider home to offer Duke a professional contract. His visit set off a small crisis for Florence Snider and her son. The United States had entered World

War II in 1941, and Ward Snider was thousands of miles away, serving with the U.S. Navy in the South Pacific. Florence Snider had to make the decision about Duke's immediate future. She had strong reservations about her son's leaving home at the tender age of 17, but an offer of $750 to sign and a $250 monthly salary was enough to persuade her.

Duke, of course, needed no persuasion. He had been dreaming about this for years. At that time, there were no major league teams in California, and Duke had adopted the Brooklyn Dodgers as his favorite team. The 1941 World Series, which the Dodgers lost to the Yankees after an agonizing bad break in Game 6, had been the decisive experience. "Listening to the World Series on the radio in those days was as much of a national pastime as baseball itself," he later wrote. "You listened to it with your family at home over the weekend, and during the week . . . you listened every afternoon at school. You didn't have to worry about getting the teacher's permission—the teacher was usually the one who brought the radio."

In signing with the Dodgers, Duke was careful not to plan too far ahead. As soon as he was 18, he would be eligible for military service. Instead of playing for his favorite team in Ebbets Field, thousands of miles to the east, he might wind up thousands of miles to the west, joining his father in the combat zone.

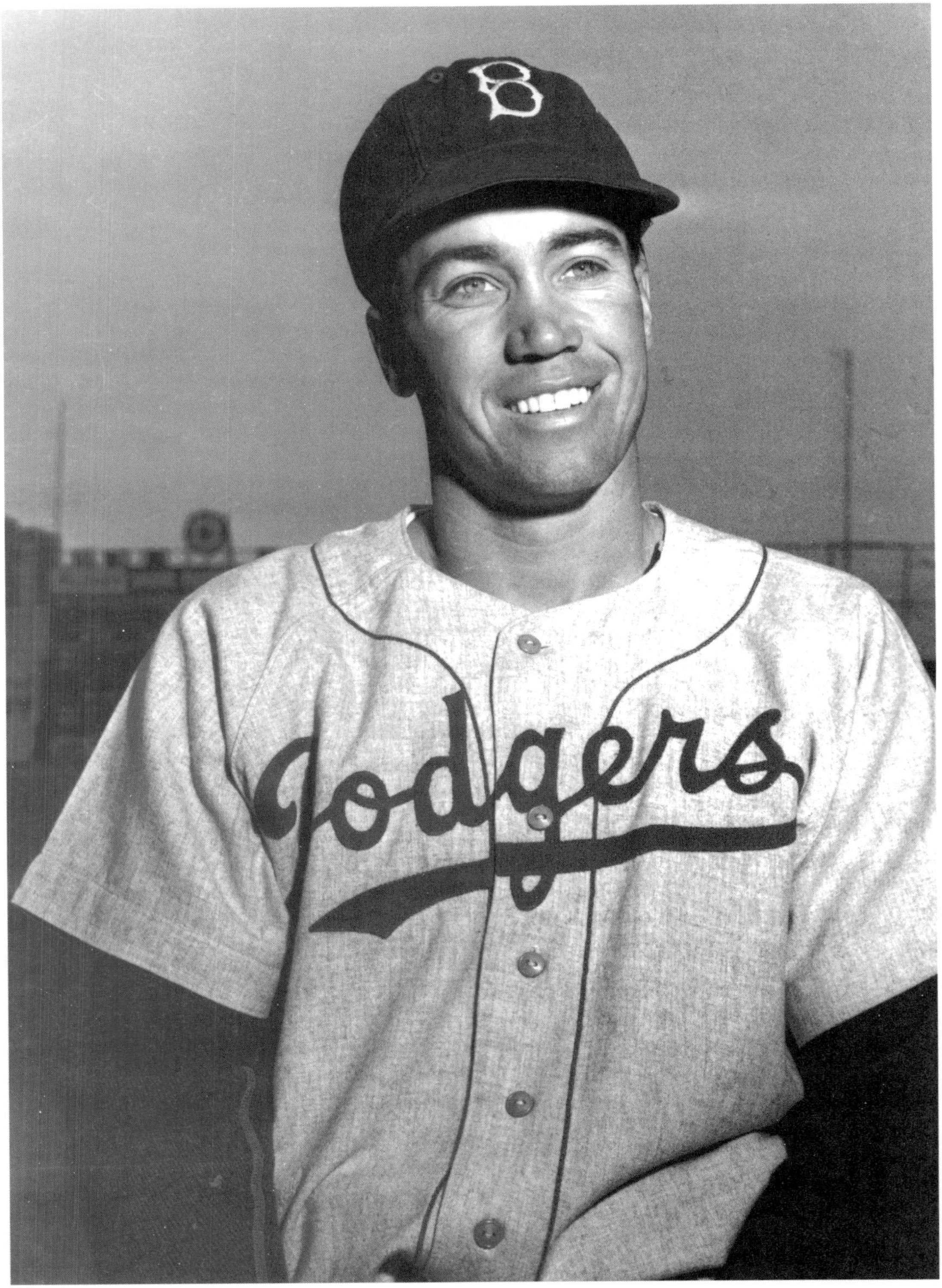
Dodgers

Duke was not going to turn 18 until September, which left him an entire summer to get a taste of professional baseball. In 1944, baseball was different than in previous years. For one thing, a number of established major leaguers were serving in the armed forces. In addition, wartime restrictions on travel made it impossible for the major league teams to train in the Florida sunshine. Thus the Dodgers found themselves preparing for the season in the chilly climate of Bear Mountain, New York. When the young Californian stepped off the train, snow was falling. "I had never seen snow and didn't own a topcoat," he recalled, "so I did a lot of running when I ventured outside."

Snider was one of hundreds of hopefuls trying to find a spot with the big club or in the minors. Even though many of his favorite Dodgers were away in the service, Snider had some colorful heroes to watch as role models during training camp: the popular outfielder Dixie Walker, a tall first baseman named Howie Schultz, and the legendary Waner brothers, Paul and Lloyd, who had starred for the Pittsburgh Pirates during the 1920s and 1930s and were finishing out their careers with Brooklyn, en route to the Hall of Fame.

With Ebbets Field's right-field wall as a backdrop, Snider poses for a publicity photo in April 1948. Snider spent most of the 1948 season improving his hitting in the minors, and by the following spring he was ready to take over as Brooklyn's starting center fielder.

As he showed his talents in training camp, the teenager from California collected his own following. New York sportswriter Red Patterson could hardly contain his enthusiasm when introducing his readers to the brightest rookie prospect in camp: "There's a seventeen-year-old, Duke Snider of Compton, California, who takes his cut at the plate a la Pete Reiser [the gifted Dodgers outfielder who led the league in 1941 with a .343 batting average] and is causing more than a slight ripple among the scouts and coaches." Yet even the most impressive rookies need seasoning, and when camp was over, Snider found himself assigned to a low-level Brooklyn farm club in Newport News, Virginia, in the Class B Piedmont League.

Snider approached his first summer of baseball away from home with a mixture of excitement and nervousness. His dream of playing as a pro was coming true, but he was not sure he would be up to the challenge. His doubts evaporated quickly as he whacked out 9 homers in the shortened three-month season—tops in the entire league. (The recycled balls being used in the minors came off the bat as if they were made of lead.) But it was not all fun and games. Along with the home runs, Snider experienced some real homesickness. There were also the stark realities of exhausting road trips in a beat-up old school bus, starvation wages of $1.75 a day in meal money, and dusty old ballparks in worse condition than the high school diamonds back home. And at the end of the summer, when he turned 18, an even larger dose of reality set in when Snider was called up for military service.

Before he faced that grim prospect, which could have put an end to his baseball career and much more, Snider had time for a last carefree month in Los Angeles, enjoying a $200 second-hand car, drive-in movies, good friends, and fast music. One special friend—his high school sweetheart, Beverly Null—would later share a larger piece of Duke's life as his wife. At the time, she could only hope for him to come back from the war.

As it turned out, World War II was a much less dangerous experience for Snider than it was for his father, who served on a ship that took part in the U.S. assaults on Japanese-held Pacific islands. The navy assigned Duke to the USS *Sperry*, a submarine tender that was stationed in the less-hazardous sectors of the South Pacific.

Snider even got to play some baseball in the navy. Now and then he faced an established major leaguer, such as Cincinnati's Johnny Vander Meer, the only pitcher in baseball history to pitch back-to-back no-hitters. Most often, though, he was washing dishes in the ship's galley, where he kept his arm in shape by slinging the really dirty items through a porthole into the Pacific. The big excitement for the *Sperry*'s crew during their months at sea was the foolproof con game they pulled on visiting submarine crews. The sailors would get up a ballgame, and Snider's shipmates would mention that he could throw the ball from one end of the sub to another, a good 300 feet. The submariners were ready to bet that he could not, and Snider's phenomenal arm, which could hurl a baseball as far as 400 feet, earned a steady income for him and the rest of the crew.

The war ended in the fall of 1945, and by the time Americans were celebrating their first post-

Jackie Robinson signs autographs for young fans before an exhibition game in April 1947. When Robinson broke baseball's color line by joining the Dodgers for the 1947 season, Snider was one of his main supporters: he had competed against Robinson in high school and was awed by his fellow Californian's ability.

war Independence Day, Snider was out of the navy and back on the ballfield. Based on his 1944 season, the Dodgers had moved him up to their Class AA team at Fort Worth, Texas. When he first reported there on July 4, 1946, however, it was all too clear that his timing was shot and his swing was rusty. But not for long. Before the season ended, Snider had hit his stride—and just about anything the Texas League pitchers could throw at him. The Fort Worth Cats won the league championship, and Snider won an invitation to spring training with the Dodgers in 1947.

Snider had firmly established himself in the plans of the Brooklyn front office. At one point,

Dodgers general manager Branch Rickey proudly informed the press that his ballclub would not even take $100,000 for their hot prospect. That was big money in those days, and Snider had every right to feel pumped up with confidence as he looked forward to the 1947 season.

As it turned out, Snider was practically ignored at the Dodgers spring training camp in Havana, Cuba. The big story of the spring was Jackie Robinson's bid to become the first black ballplayer of the 20th century to play on a major league team. Baseball was about to break out of its shameful period of racial intolerance, and not only the baseball world but the entire nation was watching Robinson as he paved the way for baseball's integration. The Dodgers had gone to Havana instead of their usual training site at Vero Beach, Florida, precisely to shield Robinson from excess publicity as he prepared to make history. But the Robinson story was just too hot, and the media even mobbed him in Cuba. As a result, Snider was able to make his own progress that spring without the overblown publicity that so often kills off a young rookie by setting up impossible expectations.

Snider was thrilled to be with the Dodgers, playing alongside such boyhood favorites as Pee Wee Reese, the team's captain and shortstop. And he had no objection to standing in the shadow of Jackie Robinson. In fact, Snider had discovered Robinson long before 1947. They were fellow Californians, and Robinson had been a star athlete at nearby Pasadena Junior College when Snider was still in junior high. "Five or six of us kids saw him play a baseball game," Snider recalled, "leave in the middle of it with his uniform still on to trot over and compete in the broad jump in a track meet, and then run back and finish the baseball game just as if nothing unusual had happened." When several Dodgers players circulated a petition before spring training began, protesting the club's plans to bring Robinson to the majors, Snider refused to sign.

Snider got another thrill at spring training when he received his first big league uniform. Rookies are usually assigned a high number, but Snider timidly requested number 4 from equipment manager John Griffin. This was the number he had always worn—it had belonged to his childhood idol, the great New York Yankees first baseman Lou Gehrig. Griffin informed Snider that the number had also been worn by his own personal favorite, Dolf Camilli, a Dodgers star of the 1930s. Griffin had not let anyone wear that number since Camilli retired. But the veteran clubhouse manager sensed there was something special about Snider and honored the rookie's request.

The Dodgers' new number 4 soon had a host of new friends among his teammates. The closest was his roommate, a strapping ex-marine from Indiana named Gil Hodges, who broke in as a catcher that same year. It that era, players usually lived close to the ballpark; the two rookies—each earning the minimum salary of $5,000—would walk the several blocks from their apartment to Ebbets Field, talking baseball every step of the way. Pee Wee Reese, the undisputed leader of the team on and off the field, was also a major influence on Snider. Snider later stated that knowing Reese and playing on the same team with him was one of the great blessings of his life.

Gil Hodges, who also broke in with the Dodgers in 1947, quickly became one of Snider's closest friends. The two rookies shared an apartment during their first season and talked base- ball night and day.

Despite Reese's many pointers and his own talent, Snider could not crack the Dodgers lineup in 1947, and the team sent him down to the minors so that he could play every day. He was called back at the end of the season, but he was not eligible to play in the World Series, which turned out to be another heartbreaker for the Dodgers—the Yankees edged them out, 4 games to 3. During the off-season, Snider returned to California, where he worked on a road-building crew and delivered mail to supple- ment his meager baseball salary. On October 25, he and Beverly Null were married in Compton's Lynwood Methodist Church. They settled in Brooklyn in time for the 1948 season, but Snider played only 53 games with the big club. He spent most of his time with the Montreal Royals, the top Dodgers farm team.

Snider might have lost heart, but the Dodgers management made it clear that they believed in him. During spring training in 1948, Branch Rickey had made the young slugger his personal project, working alone with him and hitting coach George Sisler for an hour each day. Under Rickey's expert tutelage, Snider gradually learned the strike zone and cured his habit of lunging at the ball. The work paid off in Montreal, as Snider batted over .300, with 21 homers in only 76 games. "Of all the people I have to thank," he wrote in 1988, "I'd say

Snider makes a leaping grab of a Joe DiMaggio drive during Game 5 of the 1949 World Series. Despite his sparkling play in the field, Snider got only 3 hits in 21 at-bats during the Series; his failure at the plate haunted him until the 1952 Series, when he proved that he could perform under postseason pressure.

Mr. Rickey is the one most responsible for my being in the Hall of Fame today."

Snider was finally ready to be a Brooklyn mainstay in 1949, when he won the starting job in center field and batted .292, with 23 homers and 92 RBIs. His most memorable moment occurred on the season's final day. The setting was Philadelphia's Shibe Park, where the Dodgers needed a victory over the Phillies to edge out the St. Louis Cardinals for the National League pennant. With the game tied in the 10th inning and Reese on second base, Snider drilled a line drive off Phillies reliever Ken Heintzelman that sent home the winning tally and thrilled the hometown fans so much that 25,000 of them converged on New York's Penn Station and mobbed the Dodgers when they got off their train.

For all the excitement of his first championship season, however, 1949 would end in bitter disappointment for Snider. The 1949 World Series was a week-long nightmare for him, as he went 3-for-21 at the plate. By Series end he had tied a long-standing record by striking out eight times.

Back home in California, Snider's loyal friends and relatives gave him a hero's welcome. There was a gala parade and a banquet to honor the first athlete from Compton ever to appear in a World Series. Though he was touched by the welcome and delighted by the birth of his first child, Kevin, on November 4, Snider felt like anything but a hero during the off-season. At his banquet, he had told his friends and relatives, "I promise you that if I ever get into another [Series], it will be a different story." Before long, he would have his chance to keep the promise.

4

WILLIE, MICKEY, AND THE DUKE

Baseball was front-page news in New York City during the 1950s, and each of the city's three major league teams boasted a future Hall of Famer out in center field. When compared to Mickey Mantle of the Yankees and Willie Mays of the Giants (both of whom broke into the majors in 1951), Snider often ran third—except, of course, in Brooklyn. Mantle was the darling of the press corps, heir apparent to the great Yankee tradition of Babe Ruth, Lou Gehrig, and Joe DiMaggio. And Mays was a rare phenomenon, a powerful slugger with awesome speed, a magical glove, and a cannon for an arm. But Dodgers fans were convinced that Snider never got a fair shake from the New York baseball writers—just as the entire borough of Brooklyn never got a fair shake. The press and cinema always conveyed the idea that the citizens of the city's largest borough spoke a foreign language known as Brooklynese, while the sports pages fostered an image of Snider as a sore loser.

Even his biggest fans had to admit that Snider was not perfect, at least not in the early years. While he showed almost unlimited potential with his outfield speed, potent throwing, and long-ball slugging, Snider was a free swinger who struck out frequently (a league-leading 92

Mickey Mantle (left) and Willie Mays pose for photographers during the 1951 World Series between the Yankees and the Giants. Along with Snider, Mantle and Mays gave New York a trio of incomparable center fielders; among them, the three Hall of Famers slugged 1,603 career home runs.

29

times in 1949). And when he struck out, he often sulked and fretted, which then affected his play in the field as well.

Mantle struck out even more often than Snider, and in his early seasons he was often shaky in the outfield. But Mantle's shy Oklahoma manner and his association with the seemingly invincible Yankees shielded him from heavy criticism. Snider, on the other hand, often had to bear the burden of his team's near misses. That was the case during the 1949 World Series, and the trend continued for the next two seasons as well. In 1950, the Dodgers lost the pennant to the surprising Phillies on the final day of the season when Dick Sisler smacked a dramatic 10th-inning home run. The inning before, Snider had stroked a single that seemed a sure bet to send Cal Abrams home from second base with the winning run. But Abrams stumbled rounding third, and Philadelphia outfielder Richie Ashburn nailed him with a perfect throw to the plate.

The finale of the following season was even more devastating for Snider, the Dodgers, and the entire borough of Brooklyn. After frittering away a 13½-game lead, the Dodgers ended the season tied with the surging Giants, and the bitter crosstown rivals hooked up in a special three-game playoff. In the ninth inning of the third and deciding game, the Dodgers appeared to have the pennant locked up, only to be beaten by Bobby Thomson's historic three-run homer, known ever after as "the shot heard round the world." As Thomson's low line drive sailed into the left-field seats at the Polo Grounds, it was Snider who stood poised at the wall, waiting for a carom that never came.

To their credit, the Dodgers came back strong to take the pennant in both 1952 and 1953. Snider achieved some personal vindication in both World Series. In 1952, he was the undisputed star of the Series, and the following year he was only slightly less brilliant, batting .320 with 3 home runs and 5 RBIs in 6 games. But both times, the Yankees walked off with the world championship.

Snider had his own opinion on the Willie-Mickey-Duke controversy: he thought that Joe

As Brooklyn's Jackie Robinson (42) stands rigid with shock, and losing pitcher Ralph Branca trudges off in despair, Giants players and coaches mob Bobby Thomson after his ninth-inning, three-run homer in the deciding game of the 1951 National League playoff.

DiMaggio had been the best center fielder in New York baseball history. For the rest, he claimed that neither he, Mays, nor Mantle had any real interest in the comparison game: "We used to joke about it. We knew we were creating good box office for our teams, and in every city where we played. . . . I'd run into Willie and he'd say, 'Hey, Duke, I got twelve points on you,' and I'd say, 'Yeah, but I'm leading you by fifteen RBIs.' "

In a scene from a bygone baseball era, Snider is greeted by his five-year-old son, Kevin, after a stroll to the local deli in June 1955. Though he was by now a genuine superstar, Snider was far from wealthy; he and his family lived comfortably but simply in Brooklyn's Fort Hamilton section.

New York fans tossed those numbers back and forth with a lot more passion, because each team's fans were naturally convinced that their center fielder was the best. By the time all three players were retired, most fans and commentators agreed that Mays had been incomparable, simply the best all-around player of his era. He finished his career with 660 home runs, 1,902 RBIs, and a .302 batting average (in addition to 2,062 runs scored and 338 stolen bases, phenomenal figures for a home run hitter). Mantle finished with 536 homers, 1,509 RBIs, and a .298 average; Snider weighed in with 407 home runs, 1,333 RBIs, and a .295 lifetime average. Thus, the figures put Snider in third place.

However, from 1951 through 1957, after which the Dodgers and Giants moved to the West Coast, Snider had the edge in the battle of the New York center fielders. During those seven years, he averaged 36 home runs, 111 RBIs, and a .304 batting mark. Mantle was a close second in the power category, with 29.5 home runs and 109 RBIs, though he led in batting average with .313. Mays, who spent most of 1952 and all of 1953 in the U.S. Army, averaged 26 home runs, 72 RBIs, and batted .257—in essence, he was just getting warmed up.

Thus, Brooklyn fans were hardly off base when they argued loud and long that their beloved Duke was number one. True, he never cracked the 50-home-run barrier, as Mays did in 1954, and never won the coveted Triple Crown, as Mantle did in his spectacular 1956 season. But Snider had many impressive achievements to his credit. For example, for three straight seasons (1953–55) he topped the National League in runs scored. Then, in 1957, he tied Ralph Kiner's league mark by hitting 40 or more homers for the fifth season running.

Throughout the same period, Snider and his old roommate, Gil Hodges, formed one of the great one-two hitting punches in the major leagues. Few righty-lefty power combos before or since have done so much damage to opposing pitchers. For 15 seasons, the potent pair assaulted league hurlers for a total of 745 home runs. In the end, Snider and Hodges would form the third-best homer combination in National League history. Only the Hank Aaron–Eddie Mathews and Willie Mays–Willie McCovey tandems were able to top them.

Though Snider more than justified the loyalty of the Ebbets Field faithful, he eventually drew criticism even in Brooklyn. The major incident occurred in 1955, when Snider blasted the fans for booing him and his teammates after the Dodgers lost a double-header to the Cincinnati Reds. "The Brooklyn fans are the worst in the league," he angrily told reporters in the locker room. "They don't deserve a pennant." Not surprisingly, huge headlines quoting Snider's words appeared in the morning papers. Snider reported to Ebbets Field that night prepared for an even worse booing—and the fans let him have it. He struck out his first time up, but later on, as he stood on first base after rapping out his third straight hit, the fans were on their feet, giving him a standing ovation. Like Snider himself, Brooklyn fans could be hotheaded and emotional. But they were always ready to forgive their most cherished heroes.

As Snider had pointed out to the press, the

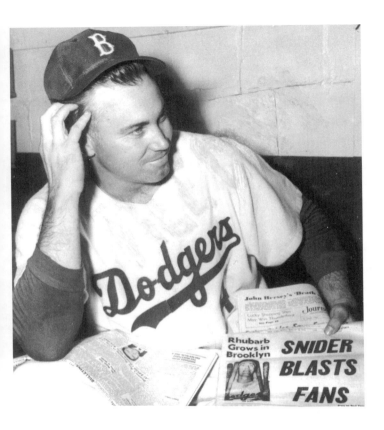

Scanning the daily news-papers before game time on August 26, 1955, Snider appears puzzled by the furor over his criticism of Brooklyn fans. Many fans booed him when he took the field that night, but after he rapped out three straight hits, the Brooklyn faithful gave their beloved Duke a standing ovation.

fans had certainly overreacted to the double-header loss, because the Dodgers were still 11 games in first place. They more than kept up the pace, winning the pennant by a 13½-game mar-gin over the Milwaukee Braves. And on the after-noon of October 4, they had the Brooklyn faithful literally dancing in the streets.

5

SUBWAY SERIES

The Brooklyn Dodgers of the early and mid-1950s were plagued with the reputation of a team that always fell short in October. Though they were, year in and year out, the most consistent team in the National League, they had to settle for being the number two team in New York City, the favorite victims of the powerful New York Yankees under manager Casey Stengel. In what became popularly known as the Subway Series, the Yankees and Dodgers met six times in World Series play between 1947 and 1956, and only once could Brooklyn muster a win. While the Yankees reigned invincible, the cry for Brooklyn fans was always "Wait until next year!"

Despite their anguish nearly every October, Brooklynites were justly proud of their beloved Bums, as the Dodgers were affectionately known. A third-place finish in 1948 (7½ games behind Boston) represents the only summer between 1946 and 1956 that the Dodgers were not serious contenders going into the season's final week. Victories on the final day of the 1946, 1950, and 1951 campaigns would have given Brooklyn an unheard-of 9 pennants in 11 seasons—one more than the Yankees actually won during that same period.

Snider jumps for joy after the final out of Game 1 of the 1952 World Series, as the Dodgers nail down a 4–2 victory over the Yankees. Despite Snider's personal heroics in the Series, the Yankees came away with a seven-game triumph and their fourth consecutive world championship.

But mere numbers cannot tell the Dodgers story. This was also one of the most colorful, star-studded teams ever assembled. Duke Snider, Roy Campanella, Gil Hodges, Pee Wee Reese, Jackie Robinson, Carl Furillo, Billy Cox, Jim Gilliam, Don Newcombe, Joe Black, Carl Erskine, Preacher Roe, Clem Labine: their 1950s rosters read like an all-time all-star team, including four eventual Hall of Famers and several more players with Hall of Fame ability who have so far fallen short of the votes required for enshrinement at Cooperstown.

Even the great 1950s Yankees squads led by Mickey Mantle, Yogi Berra, Phil Rizzuto, Elston Howard, Gil McDougald, Hank Bauer, Gene Woodling, Joe Collins, Billy Martin, and others could not stack up against the Dodgers starting lineup. But the Dodgers fell short in baseball's most crucial department—pitching. When the two teams went head-to-head, the Yankees always had at least one more reliable hurler to call on when the chips were down. The most glaring example of Brooklyn's deficiency was the 1952 World Series, when the Dodgers were forced to use Joe Black, their ace reliever, as a starting pitcher in three games. Black pitched heroically, posting a 2.53 ERA in 21 innings of work, but he could not single-handedly overcome the New York duo of Reynolds and Raschi. Moreover, with Black in a starting role, the Dodgers had no one reliable left in their bullpen, whereas the Yankees were able to call on Eddie Lopat and Bob Kuzava, who had combined for 18 wins during the season.

The 1952 Series is perhaps best remembered for the agony of Gil Hodges, who, despite 32

homers and 102 RBIs in the regular season, went 0-for-21 in the Series and had people lighting candles for him in Brooklyn's churches. Even without Hodges's bat, the Dodgers won Games 1, 3, and 5 of the Series, including two of three games played at Yankee Stadium, but the Yankees roared back with two final victories in Ebbets Field. Even Snider's record-tying 4 homers could not save the Dodgers from their sixth straight World Series defeat.

Hodges redeemed himself in the 1953 Series with a .364 average, but the Yankees triumphed again, 4 games to 2, as the usually light-hitting

Brooklyn's representatives on the 1952 National League All-Star team pose for a photo at Ebbets Field: (left to right) Carl Furillo, Jackie Robinson, Roy Campanella, Pee Wee Reese, Snider, Preacher Roe, and Gil Hodges. The league's best team by far, the Dodgers captured six pennants between 1947 and 1956 and narrowly missed winning two more.

Billy Martin batted .500, with 12 base hits and 8 RBIs. In Game 4, which the Dodgers won 7–3, Snider contributed 4 RBIs with 2 doubles and a home run.

Rebounding from his disaster in 1949, Snider made his next four World Series a showcase for his talents. Although the Dodgers defeated their crosstown rivals only once, Snider never had to take a back seat to his own personal rival, Mickey Mantle. While Mantle blasted 8 home runs and knocked in 17 runs in the four World Series, Snider racked up 10 homers and 24 RBIs of his own. Snider batted .345 in the 1952 Series and .320 in 1953. Mantle also batted .345 in 1952, but he fell off to a lackluster .208 the following year. The debate might rage on about the best center fielder in New York during the summer months, but Snider was the hands-down winner when it came to Series play.

The 1954 season was a truly great one for Snider, perhaps the finest all-around performance of his career. His batting average zoomed to .341, only 4 points behind Mays for the National League batting championship, and he led the league in total bases. He tied Gil Hodges for second place in RBIs with 130 and tied the Cardinals' Stan Musial for the league lead in runs scored. In addition, he was second in base hits and slugging average.

Unfortunately, the 1954 Dodgers did not do nearly as well as a team. Willie Mays was out of the army and back in the Polo Grounds, and his brilliant play took the Giants all the way to the pennant. Under new manager Walter Alston, Brooklyn finished 5 games behind. (To make the defeat even more bitter for Brooklyn fans, the

Giants then went on to win the World Series, upsetting a splendid Cleveland Indians team that had won 111 games.) It was beginning to look as if the glory years might have passed for Snider and his teammates without a single championship crown.

But the Dodgers were not about to give up. They shot from the starting gate in 1955 with a 10-game winning streak and then posted 22 triumphs in their first 24 contests. By the end of April, the Bums were already 9 games ahead of second-place Milwaukee, and they never looked back for the remainder of that runaway season.

While Snider's 42 home runs put him behind Mays (51), Cincinnati's Ted Kluszewski (47), and Chicago's Ernie Banks (44), he was the league champ in runs batted in (136) as well as runs scored (126), and he stood high among the leaders in slugging percentage, total bases, and bases on balls. And once again, he saved his very best stuff for the World Series.

The first two games took place at Yankee Stadium, and after the Yankees took both contests, the press was ready to write off the Dodgers again. "We had a different attitude," recalled Snider, who had hit a mammoth home run into the stadium's third deck during Game 1. "The Yankees never really clobbered us in those previous World Series. We felt we were at least their equal, and in our more candid moments we thought we were probably better."

With that attitude, the Dodgers roared back with three emphatic victories at Ebbets Field, 8–3, 8–5, and 5–3. Snider won Game 4 with a three-run homer in the fifth inning and blasted two solo shots in Game 5. Back in the Bronx, the

World champions at last, the jubilant Dodgers converge on Johnny Podres after the left-hander's 2–0 shutout of the Yankees in Game 7 of the 1955 World Series. Sparking the Dodgers with his potent bat, Snider became the first player in history to hit four home runs in two separate World Series.

Yankees captured the sixth game, setting the stage for another epic confrontation. At this point, Snider was hobbled by a sore knee, which he had wrenched when he stepped on a sprinkler head in the Yankee Stadium outfield. He had gotten the Dodgers within range, and they went the rest of the way on their own. Left-hander Johnny Podres blanked the Yanks on 8 hits, Gil Hodges drove in 2 runs, and Sandy Amoros snuffed out the Yankees' sixth-inning rally with a miraculous running catch in the left-field corner. When Pee Wee Reese fielded Gil McDougald's grounder and threw to Hodges for the final out, the entire borough of Brooklyn exploded with joy. People ran out of their houses to celebrate, and all through the night spontaneous victory parades snaked through the borough's teeming neighborhoods.

Snider, who became the only man in history to hit 4 home runs in two separate World Series, got another warm welcome from his friends and family back in California, and this time there was nothing bittersweet about it. He had come home as a world champion.

Brooklyn
soft collars on
Heusen
Shirts
...ever !
AMERICA RUNS ON BULOV
1954 '54

When I saw Ebbets Field for the first time as a Brooklyn Dodger, it was love at first sight," Snider later recalled. "I loved that old ballpark and everything about it, and that covered a lot!" Many of Snider's fondest memories concerned the fans, some of whom were almost as well known as the players: "There was Hilda Chester with her cowbell in the outfield stands. There was a fan named Eddie Battan who used to blow a tin whistle. The Sym-Phony band strolled the stands playing Dixieland music, and from his seat Jack Pierce sent up balloons with Cookie Lavagetto's name on them, because Cookie was his favorite player." But Snider had more than the friendly fans in mind when he sang the praises of Ebbets Field. He also remembered the ballpark's friendly right-field wall, which was only 297 feet from home plate at the foul line and a mere 335 feet away in right-center.

Because the left-field and center-field seats were also within easy reach, the Dodgers had developed an awesome array of right-handed batters. As a result, the Dodgers almost never saw left-handers, at least not at Ebbets Field. This allowed Snider to feed off a steady diet of right-handed pitching, ideal for his graceful southpaw swing, and from 1952 through

Snider makes a practice leap against Ebbets Field's storied right-field wall in July 1954. Though Snider loved playing in the cozy Brooklyn ballpark, the field's tight dimensions often prevented him from showing off his range and speed in the outfield.

1956, he amassed 40 or more homers each season.

Snider's critics made much of his apparent luck in landing with the right team in the right ballpark. In his own defense, Snider has pointed out quite correctly that Yankee Stadium was even more favorable to left-handed power hitters: the right-field seats were just as close to home plate, and they were fronted by a barrier only 4 feet high, as opposed to the towering 40-foot wall of Ebbets Field. Had Snider played for the Yankees, he might have hit even more home runs, because many of the shots that he hit high off the wall at Ebbets Field would have landed in the seats at Yankee Stadium.

In one way, Ebbets Field worked against Snider. The park's tight dimensions made it hard for him to show off his skills as an outfielder. Mantle and Mays, playing in ballparks with vast open spaces in center field, left-center, and right-center, had the chance to make spectacular running catches. Perhaps more than anything in his career, Mays is remembered for his astonishing over-the-shoulder grab of the mammoth blast hit by Vic Wertz at the Polo Grounds in Game 1 of the 1954 World Series. Snider had no opportunity to run down shots like that in Ebbets Field—he could only turn and watch them leave the ballpark. In order to play center field at home, he had to master the art of judging fly balls, knowing when to go for the catch and when to position himself to field a carom off the wall. Snider did this so flawlessly that people were often fooled into thinking that it took no special talent.

All in all, Snider could not have asked for anything more than playing in Ebbets Field. Even though he was a native Californian, he was

*The Dodgers Sym-Phony,
a homegrown Dixieland
band, was a colorful fea-
ture of the Brooklyn baseball scene. The Ebbets
Field fans knew how to
have fun, but they also
took their baseball very
seriously: in their eyes, the
talented, scrappy, often
underrated Dodgers
embodied the spirit of
Brooklyn.*

no less heartbroken than the people of Brooklyn
when the Dodgers announced that they were
moving to Los Angeles after the 1957 season. "I
hit a home run onto Bedford Avenue on the
Sunday afternoon of our last weekend in Ebbets
Field," Snider recalled. "It would be the last
home run anyone ever hit there. After the game,
I told Walt Alston I didn't want to play the next
two-game series against Pittsburgh. . . . I'd hit a
home run . . . and I wanted to remember that as
my last Ebbets Field experience. I was being torn
away from my baseball home, and I wanted to
remember her that way. Walt understood." A few
years later, when Duke and Bev Snider saw the
photos of the old ballpark being demolished,
they broke down and cried.

Snider had another shock in April 1958,
when the Dodgers—now wearing the letters *LA*
on their blue caps instead of the old familiar *B*—
first arrived at the Los Angeles Coliseum for
their opening West Coast home game. Their
opponents that day were the Giants, who had
relocated to San Francisco. None of the players
had previously seen the huge oval stadium's
strange dimensions for baseball: a 40-foot-high
screen in left field stood only 251 feet from home

plate, but the right-field fence appeared to be in the next county—the distance to right-center was 440 feet. Right-handed sluggers such as Gil Hodges might now dream of challenging Babe Ruth's single-season homer record, but for southpaws like Snider, the future looked bleak.

As Snider came out of the runway that first April afternoon, he was confronted by an excited Willie Mays, who loved to put the needle in opposing players. "Look where that right-field fence is, Duke!" Mays shouted. "They sure fixed you up good. You couldn't reach that wall with a cannon. You're done, man! They just took your bat away from you."

The good-hearted Mays was not really gleeful about Snider's predicament, but his analysis was right on the money. Snider's first year on the West Coast marked the beginning of the end of his glorious power-hitting career. He had no choice but to change his swing and hit the ball to all fields instead of trying to pull everything. As a result, he hit .300 for the first time in three years. In Los Angeles, the man who had hit 40 or

An aerial view of the Los Angeles Coliseum on April 18, 1958, with 78,672 people on hand to witness the first Dodgers game on the West Coast. The outfield dimensions show why the Coliseum was a paradise for right-handed power hitters and a nightmare for left-handers such as Snider.

more homers for five straight summers could now only manage 15. Snider's RBI total sank from 92 to 58. To make matters worse, a series of injuries limited his playing time to 106 games.

The Dodgers as a whole fared even worse, sinking to seventh place in 1958. The following season, general manager Buzzie Bavasi began to rebuild the Dodgers, concentrating on pitching and speed. By the time he was done, the only former Brooklyn stars who remained in the starting lineup were Gilliam, Hodges, and Snider. Shifting over to right field in place of the ailing Carl Furillo, Snider rebounded with an excellent season, batting .308 with 23 home runs and 88 RBIs. Better still, the Dodgers surprised the baseball world with an upset pennant victory, coming from behind to tie the Milwaukee Braves in the final weeks and then taking a special playoff at season's end.

In the World Series against the Chicago White Sox, an aching knee reduced Snider to pinch-hitting status until Game 6. At that point, the Dodgers had a 3–2 lead in games, but they were about to face Early Wynn, the tough right-hander who had shut them out in Game 1. Snider convinced Alston to put him in the lineup, and in the third inning he hit a two-run homer to the opposite field, breaking a scoreless tie and sparking the Dodgers to an eventual 9–3 victory. It was Snider's 11th World Series home run, a total that had only been surpassed by Babe Ruth's 15. (During the next few years, both Mickey Mantle and Yogi Berra were to pass Snider on the all-time Series home run list.) For the second time ever, Snider and his Dodgers were world champions. But this time there were no parades in Brooklyn.

WAITING FOR GLORY

Bev and Duke Snider, along with their children—Kevin, Pamela, and Kurt (left to right)—share the limelight on Duke Snider Night at the Los Angeles Coliseum, August 26, 1960. During the festivities, Snider was honored as the greatest slugger in Dodgers history.

Snider's 1959 World Series home run—hit, significantly, in Comiskey Park rather than the Los Angeles Coliseum—turned out to be his last great moment as a Dodgers slugger. In 1960, he appeared in only 101 games, batting a disappointing .243 with 14 home runs and just 36 RBIs. The following year he played in fewer than 100 games for the first time since his rookie campaign and wound up with 16 homers and 56 RBIs while batting .296. And by 1962, his stats were down to 5 home runs and 30 RBIs in 80 games.

The real evidence that Snider's career was winding down came in 1963, when the Dodgers sold his contract to a hopeless expansion team—the New York Mets. The Mets had just completed their first season in the league under former Yankees manager Casey Stengel, losing more games (120) than any team in baseball history. They may well have been the worst team to ever appear in the major leagues. It was hardly the place for a proud champion to spend the final days of his career. In fact, when Snider heard the news of the sale, he called Buzzie Bavasi and said that he was going to retire. Bavasi argued against the move, reminding Snider how close he was to some cherished career milestones. "Go to New York and get your 400 home runs and 2,000 hits," the general manager counseled, and in later years Snider was happy that he took his friend's advice.

Snider also took some consolation in the fact that he would be spending his last baseball days in good company: Gil Hodges, Roger Craig, Charlie Neal, Tim Harkness, Larry Burright, and Norm Sherry—all former Dodgers—were now wearing the Mets uniform. Another plus for Snider was the chance to play once more in New York City, the scene of so many past glories.

Snider later described his first Mets appearance at the old Polo Grounds as one of the most emotional moments of his career. "As I came out onto the outfield grass and started walking toward the infield," Snider recalled, "the first few fans who saw me started applauding, and the noise seemed to build with each step I took. I was getting goose pimples. Everyone was being so nice to this old Dodger!"

Indeed, a legendary hero had returned home. And New York fans—among the most knowledgeable and enthusiastic in all of baseball—had not forgotten the great moments Snider had given them in the past. A series of homemade banners strung on the outfield walls seemed to sum up the fans' feelings that day. One read, "It's Worth the Loot to Get the Duke" (the Mets had paid a reported $40,000), and another simply said "Welcome Home, Snider—We Still Love You!"

The season with the cellar-dwelling Mets was not a total loss for Snider. Although his team wound up with a disastrous 51-111 record, at least Snider got a chance to play. In 129 games, he managed to hit double figures in home runs,

Mets fans at the Polo Grounds welcome Snider back to New York in April 1963. Accustomed to playing for winners, Snider suffered through a dreadful 111-loss season with the National League expansion team, but he did experience the thrill of reaching the 400-home-run milestone.

and he finally reached the milestone of 400 career round-trippers. Snider's achievement failed to get the attention it might have in different circumstances, because the press clearly had a hard time taking anything a Met did seriously. It was hardly surprising that teammate Jimmy Piersall grabbed bigger headlines when he smacked his 100th career homer a few days later and celebrated by running around the bases backward.

After the season, Snider decided that he could not endure another season of 100-plus losses and asked the Mets to trade him, if possible to a contender. The Mets obliged, and at the start of the 1964 season, Snider flew west to join his new ballclub—the San Francisco Giants. He was so happy to be back with a winning team that he completely missed the irony of the situation. It only hit him when he suited up in the Giants clubhouse and caught sight of himself in the mirror: he could hardly believe he was wearing the uniform so despised by the old Dodgers and the Ebbets Field fans. But he also realized that he and his wife had four growing children— Kurt, Pam, Kevin, and Dawna—to support. So, perhaps for the first time in his long career, Snider would truly play more for a paycheck than for the pure love of the game.

After an unhappy and unproductive year with the Giants (4 home runs, 17 RBIs, and a .210 average in 91 games), the 37-year-old Snider received an offer to return to the Dodgers organization as a minor league manager. He took the job, but managing proved frustrating. Playing baseball had always come easily to Snider; it was much harder work teaching the finer points of the game to youngsters with far less talent and promise than he. Nevertheless, Snider stayed with it and even brought his ballclubs home in first place in three out of his four seasons on the job.

Unfortunately, even successful minor league managers do not make large sums of money. As a star player, Snider had commanded $40,000—well below the major league minimum in the 1990s but a substantial sum in the early 1960s. His manager's salary, on the other hand, was only $12,000 a year; even with the help of some investments Snider had made during his playing days, he and his wife were constantly worried about money. Looking back, he credited Bev Snider's astute financial management with pulling the family through.

By 1969, Snider was out of baseball entirely, tending bar at a California restaurant he had bought into. Quite unexpectedly, he received a call from John McHale, general manager of the Montreal Expos. McHale had heard Snider do some color commentary on San Diego Padres telecasts, and he offered Snider a steady job in that capacity with the Expos. Snider accepted the offer, even though some might have thought it a strange career move for someone who had often had run-ins with the media throughout his playing career. But Snider's passion for the game and his willingness to speak his mind made him an entertaining TV analyst, and his career in the broadcast booth stretched out for 14 seasons—almost as long as his career on the diamond.

Shortly after Snider began his broadcasting career, he became eligible for the Baseball Hall of Fame. His 407 home runs, 2,116 hits, 1,333 RBIs, and .295 lifetime batting average certainly made him a worthy candidate, if not a surefire selection. But year after year, he failed to receive the needed votes. "At first I didn't think too

Joined by fellow Hall of Famer Mickey Mantle, Snider autographs copies of his autobiography during a 1988 publicity session at Mantle's New York restaurant. After retiring as a player, Snider spent 14 seasons as a broadcaster for the Montreal Expos.

much about it," Snider remembered, "but when the media keep bringing it up year after year it truly began to trouble me."

In January 1980, the long-awaited call finally came from Jack Lang, the president of the Baseball Writers Association of America. The writers had finally given Snider the votes he needed to enter the Hall of Fame. Duke and Beverly immediately jumped on a plane for New York, where they attended a press conference, saw old friends, and basked in the affection that

New York baseball fans still held for Brooklyn's old number 4. A few months later, when he stood on the podium at Cooperstown, New York, with his family, several old teammates, and many friends in the audience, Snider knew that all the old struggles and controversies had been put to rest. He was taking his place among the greats of the game, alongside such cherished teammates as Jackie Robinson, Roy Campanella, and Pee Wee Reese. It was now established forever that Duke Snider had been one of the finest outfielders ever to roam the pastures of America's baseball diamonds.

CHRONOLOGY

1926   Born Edwin Donald Snider in Los Angeles, California, on September 19

1944   Signs contract with Brooklyn Dodgers; begins professional career in Piedmont League with Newport News, Virginia, team; leads league in doubles and home runs

1945–46 Serves in U.S. Navy during World War II

1946   Plays Class AA ball with Fort Worth Cats in the Texas League

1947   Makes major league debut with the Dodgers but spends the bulk of the season in the minors with the Montreal Royals; marries Beverly Null on October 25

1949   Becomes starting center fielder with the Dodgers and hits 23 home runs, with 92 RBIs; plays in his first World Series but has only 3 hits and no RBIs

1952   Ties World Series record with 4 homers; also collects Series-high 10 hits

1953   Has second straight heavy-hitting World Series performance with 5 RBIs and .320 batting average

1954   Records best all-around season with .341 batting average, 40 home runs, 130 RBIs, and a league-leading 120 runs scored

1955   Leads National League in RBIs and runs scored; sets a record by hitting 4 home runs in the World Series for the second time; Dodgers win their first world championship

1956   Snider leads National League in home runs with 43

1957   Hits the last home run in the history of Ebbets Field

1958   Dodgers move to Los Angeles

1959   Snider makes final World Series appearance, posting World Series career records for a National Leaguer in home runs (11) and RBIs (26)

1962   Named team captain for final season with Dodgers; collects the first base hit in new Dodger Stadium

1963   Returns to New York as a member of the expansion New York Mets; hits 400th career home run

1964   Plays final big league season as part-time outfielder and pinch-hitter for the San Francisco Giants

1966–69 Manages various teams in the Dodgers minor league system

1970–72 Works for San Diego Padres as scout, TV analyst, and minor league manager

1974–87 Works as TV analyst for Montreal Expos

1980   Elected to National Baseball Hall of Fame

EDWIN DONALD SNIDER
"DUKE"
BROOKLYN N.L., LOS ANGELES N.L.,
NEW YORK N.L., SAN FRANCISCO N.L.,
1947 - 1964
HIT 407 CAREER HOME RUNS AND TIED N.L.
RECORD WITH 40 OR MORE ROUND-TRIPPERS
FIVE YEARS IN A ROW, 1953-1957. BATTED .300
OR BETTER SEVEN TIMES IN COMPILING .295
LIFETIME AVERAGE. TOPPED LEAGUE IN SLUG-
GING PCT. TWICE AND TOTAL BASES THREE TIMES.
FIRST TO HIT FOUR HOMERS IN A WORLD SERIES
TWICE -- IN 1952 AND 1955. SET N.L.
RECORD FOR SERIES HOMERS (11).

MAJOR LEAGUE STATISTICS

BROOKLYN DODGERS, LOS ANGELES DODGERS, NEW YORK METS, SAN FRANCISCO GIANTS

YEAR	TEAM	G	AB	R	H	2B	3B	HR	RBI	BA	SB
1947	BKN N	40	83	6	20	3	1	0	5	.241	2
1948		53	160	22	39	6	6	5	21	.244	4
1949		146	552	100	161	28	7	23	92	.292	12
1950		152	620	109	199	31	10	31	107	.321	16
1951		150	606	96	168	26	6	29	101	.277	14
1952		144	534	80	162	25	7	21	92	.303	7
1953		153	590	132	198	38	4	42	126	.336	16
1954		149	584	120	199	39	10	40	130	.341	6
1955		148	538	126	166	34	6	42	136	.309	9
1956		151	542	99	158	33	2	43	101	.292	3
1957		139	508	91	139	25	7	40	92	.274	3
1958	LA N	106	327	45	102	12	3	15	58	.312	2
1959		126	370	59	114	11	2	23	88	.308	1
1960		101	235	38	57	13	5	14	36	.243	1
1961		85	233	35	69	8	3	16	56	.296	1
1962		80	158	28	44	11	3	5	30	.278	2
1963	NY N	129	354	44	86	8	3	14	45	.243	0
1964	SF N	91	167	16	35	7	0	4	17	.210	0
Totals		2143	7161	1259	2116	358	85	407	1333	.295	99
World Series (6 years)		36	133	21	38	8	0	11	26	.286	1
All-Star Games (7 years)		7	11	3	3	1	0	0	0	.273	0

FURTHER READING

Bjarkman, Peter C. *The Brooklyn Dodgers.* New York: Chartwell Books, 1992.

———. *Baseball's Great Dynasties: The Dodgers.* New York: W. H. Smith Gallery Books, 1990.

Daley, Arthur. *Kings of the Home Run.* New York: Putnam, 1962.

Golenbock, Peter. *Bums: An Oral History of the Brooklyn Dodgers.* New York: Putnam, 1984.

Honig, Donald. *The Brooklyn Dodgers: An Illustrated Tribute.* New York: St. Martin's Press, 1981.

———. *Mays, Mantle, Snider: A Celebration.* New York: Macmillan, 1987.

Kahn, Roger. *The Boys of Summer.* New York: Harper & Row, 1972.

Reidenbaugh, Lowell. *Cooperstown: Where Baseball's Legends Live Forever.* St. Louis: Sporting News, 1983.

Snider, Duke, with Bill Gilbert. *The Duke of Flatbush.* New York: Zebra Books, 1988.

Winehouse, Irwin. *The Duke Snider Story.* New York: Julian Messner, 1964.

INDEX

RE CREDITS
de World Photos, print courtesy National Baseball Library, Cooperstown, NY: p. 47; Courtesy of Compton
unity College Library: pp. 12, 16; National Baseball Library, Cooperstown, NY: p. 60; UPI/Bettmann: pp. 2, 8,
, 22, 25, 26, 28, 31, 32 (print courtesy National Baseball Library, Cooperstown, NY), 35, 36, 39, 42, 44, 48,
, 56, 58.

PETER C. BJARKMAN also known as "Doctor Baseball," is the author of more than 20 baseball biographies and history books, including the two-volume *Encyclopedia of Major League Baseball Team Histories*, *The Baseball Scrapbook*, and *Baseball & the Game of Life: Stories for the Thinking Fan*. In addition, he has written *The History of the NBA* and the *Encyclopedia of Pro Basketball Team Histories*. Dr. Bjarkman has also taught English and linguistics at Purdue University and the University of Colorado and currently lives in Lafayette, Indiana, with his wife, Dr. Ronnie Wilbur, a college professor. He is also author of *Roberto Clemente, Ernie Banks*, and *Warren Spahn* in the Chelsea House BASEBALL LEGENDS series.

JIM MURRAY, veteran sports columnist of the *Los Angeles Times*, is one of America's most acclaimed writers. He has been named "America's Best Sportswriter" by the National Association of Sportscasters and Sportswriters 14 times, was awarded the Red Smith Award, and was twice winner of the National Headliner Award. In addition, he was awarded the J. G. Taylor Spink Award in 1987 for "meritorious contributions to baseball writing." With this award came his 1988 induction into the National Baseball Hall of Fame in Cooperstown, New York. In 1990, Jim Murray was awarded the Pulitzer Prize for Commentary.

EARL WEAVER is the winningest manager in the Baltimore Orioles' history by a wide margin. He compiled 1,480 victories in his 17 years at the helm. After managing eight different minor league teams, he was given the chance to lead the Orioles in 1968. Under his leadership the Orioles finished lower than second place in the American League East only four times in 17 years. One of only 12 managers in big league history to have managed in four or more World Series, Earl was named Manager of the Year in 1979. The popular Weaver had his number 5 retired in 1982, joining Brooks Robinson, Frank Robinson, and Jim Palmer, whose numbers were retired previously. Earl Weaver continues his association with the professional baseball scene by writing, broadcasting, and coaching.